2000
AND BEYOND

Countdown to the Millennium

DONA SMITH

A Creative Media Applications Production.
Art direction by Fabia Wargin Design.

Printed in the United States of America.

10 9 8 7 6 5 4 3 2 1

CONTENTS

THE PAST MILLENNIUM

Mil-len-ni-um. Millennium. It means a span of one thousand years or a thousandth anniversary. Today when people talk about the millennium, they usually mean the big one coming up—the year 2000.

If you find yourself still writing "1998" for a while when it's really the year 1999, you'll have to think a little harder the following year to remember to start with a *2* instead of a *1*.

Some people believe all sorts of weird things will happen at the dawn of the millennium, such as alien invasions or meteor showers. These ideas seem strange to other people, however, because the word *millennium* also means a hoped-for period of joy, prosperity, and justice. It does seem that, since we are all becoming more careful about respecting our environment and treating each other fairly, the millennium should hold some good things for us.

The first century (that is, the first one hundred years) of the next millennium will be called the twenty-first century. Rapid, wonderful changes are expected, and you'll be part of them. To imagine how many changes are likely to take place between 2000 and 2100, let's look at how far we've come in the past 100 years or so.

Lots and lots of inventions appeared during the twentieth century. People have discovered that all sorts of things they once thought were impossible *are* possible. Unfortunately, inventors are often just laughed at and their new ideas are thought to be dumb when they're first presented. Here are some products that weren't at all popular when they were invented:

✳**TELEPHONE**—When Alexander Graham Bell demonstrated his invention in 1876 at the Philadelphia Centennial Expo, most people showed little interest in the device! It took Bell several years to convince the public that the telephone was an important invention that could change their lives. Imagine what your life would have been like if he hadn't been successful!

✳**ELECTRIC LIGHTBULB**—Did you know that many people—including a former President of the United States—were once *afraid* of electric light? It's true. Electric lights were installed in the White House in 1891, but President Benjamin Harrison and his wife were so wary of electric shocks that they wouldn't touch the switches! The first couple used oil lamps or had servants turn the lights on.

✳**BICYCLE**—The first bicycle probably wasn't popular because it wasn't very practical—it didn't even have pedals! The bike consisted of two wheels, a flat board on top of them, and a steering handle. The rider had to run to gather speed, then lift his or her feet and glide. Perhaps it was easier to simply walk!

✳**TELEVISION**—Black-and-white TV—have you ever even seen it?—was invented in 1926, and color television was invented in 1928. Lots of people, including some of the owners of big Hollywood movie studios, thought television was a ridiculous idea. Well, they sure were wrong! But black-and-white TV didn't become common in homes until the 1940s. Color TVs became popular in the early 1960s.

✳**CAR**—Most people thought early cars were too hard to operate. To start the first gasoline-powered automobiles, a person had to turn a crank at the front of the car. In fact, many folks thought a big chair on wheels that looked something like a sleigh would be better than a car. When the ignition key was finally invented, however, cars became much easier to start, and their popularity soared. Now many families in the United States have two cars.

✳**MICROWAVE OVEN**—The microwave oven was invented *way* back in 1946, but it didn't catch on for years. The food it made tasted good but looked ugly. It took quite a while to get the kinks out, but now having a microwave at home is pretty common.

✳**COPY MACHINE**—Can you believe the copy machine was invented in 1938? It was regarded as a frivolous toy for a long while. It wasn't until the 1960s that people finally realized that copiers were serious time-saving office tools.

TYPEWRITER—The typewriter—which has largely been replaced today by the PC—has been around since the late nineteenth century—that is, the late 1800s—but few people back then thought it would ever be accepted. At that time, it was considered proper to handwrite letters and impolite to send something printed by a machine. In the early part of this century, sending a typewritten note may have been akin to sending junk mail today.

TEFLON—The stuff that keeps eggs from sticking to a pan was invented in the late 1930s, but it wasn't used in homes until the 1960s. Now, Teflon is used in plenty of other things besides frying pans. It's used in clothing and even in spaceships!

VIDEO GAMES—The first video game was invented in 1958, but this type of entertainment didn't really catch on until the 1970s. Go figure!

COMPUTERS—People didn't actually *laugh* at the idea of computers. Most of them didn't even know computers existed. The first one was used in the 1940s for military purposes during World War II. It was so huge that it took up a whole room. Compare that with the laptops we have today! This giant computer, called the Colossus, was used to crack enemy codes. Its existence was kept top secret until 1976.

Many twentieth-century inventions changed daily life around the world, but the computer's influence keeps growing as machines get more powerful. It makes you wonder how they will affect life in the millennium. Computers are involved in practically every aspect of society. Even if you speak to a human bank teller instead of using an ATM (Automated Teller Machine), your banking is handled by a computer at some point. Today's cars are run by computers. Stoves, refrigerators, and other home appliances are run by computers. Robots, which are also computers, are used as security guards. Even airplane pilots depend largely on computers. Your parents probably use a computer at work. You might have a computer in your house that you use to do your homework and to send e-mail to your friends. Maybe you surf the Internet.

Many computers currently have a problem that needs to be fixed before the millennium. A lot of the work that computers do for people coordinates with a timetable built into the computer. But at midnight on December 31, 1999, some computers will read the date incorrectly. The last two numbers in the year will reset to two zeros, and the computer will "think" that it is 1900—not 2000.

That's not a big problem if you're doing a book report. But it's a very big problem if you're operating airlines or managing bank accounts—or doing anything that has a timetable used by a computer, which includes almost everything. So, some inventions actually invent new kinds of problems to be solved. Luckily, computer manufacturers and programmers had the foresight to predict this problem before 1999, so they are working furiously to prevent our computers from crashing on January 1, 2000!

THE BEST INVENTIONS EVER?

Now that we've learned about some inventions that most people scoffed at, let's look at a few ideas that lots of people took seriously.

TIPPING HAT—In the early part of the twentieth century, many men wore hats. It was the custom to tip your hat when you passed a friend or an acquaintance. As you can imagine, men who knew lots of people got tired of tipping their hats. A French inventor tried to solve the problem by creating a hat rigged up with springs. When the thing was cranked up, all the wearer had to do was nod and the hat tipped itself. Can you imagine wearing something like that to school?

COOL CHAIR—You could rock and keep cool with this rocking chair. Equipped with a pump that was a little like a fan, it supposedly let you rock in comfort on hot days.

WATER WALKERS—Strap a big balloon filled with gas around your waist. Then put some things that look sort of like skis on your feet. The inventor was sure it would work like a charm. It didn't.

It's amazing what some people can dream up, isn't it? Now let's take a look at some important (or at least useful) inventions and accomplishments of the twentieth century.

1903	Airplane
1907	Household detergent
1908	Cellophane
1912	Stainless steel
1920	Commercial radio broadcasts
1921	Lie detector
1923	Frozen food
1924	Clothes washer and spin dryer
1926	Television
1927	Pop-up toaster
1928	Color television
	Penicillin
	Vitamin C
1930	Discovery of the planet Pluto
1931	Electric razor
1936	Helicopter
1937	Nylon
1938	Ballpoint pen
	Copy machine
	Teflon
1940	Radar

1945	Artificial kidney
	Vinyl floor covering
1947	Holography
1948	Velcro
1949	Jet airliner
1953	Discovery of DNA
	Measles vaccine
1957	Polio vaccine
1958	Laser
1960	Weather satellite
1961	Manned space flight
1963	Cassette tape
1969	Moon landing
1977	Space shuttle
1980	Solar-powered aircraft
1982	Artificial heart
1984	Compact disc player
	Cloning
1985	CD-ROM (compact disc read-only memory)
1986	DNA fingerprinting

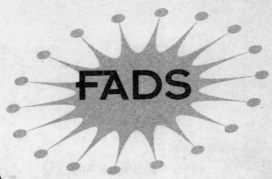

FADS

A fad is a type of clothing, a hobby, a diet, or even a way of talking that becomes wildly popular. Suddenly, everybody is wearing it, doing it, eating it, or saying it. Then, just as suddenly, the fad isn't popular anymore; it isn't so cool. Reading about fads from the past can be fun. For example, it was a fad in London around 1906 to have the picture of a favorite friend or relative put on your fingernail. And around 1800 some people thought it was cool to unwrap a mummy for their friends at a dinner party. Yes, it's true!

Here are a few more fads that came and went (and often came and went again) during the 1900s.

*Short skirts
*Drive-in movies
*Poodle skirts
*Miniature golf
*The grunge look
*Platform shoes

*Free dishes for customers at movie theaters and gas stations
*Mood rings
*Go-go boots
*Bell-bottomed pants

Are you ready to blast off into the next millennium? Let's go! But first, take some time to imagine what *you* think the inventions and fads of tomorrow might be.

Important INVENTIONS
I think will happen in the next century:

_____

_____

_____

_____

_____

_____

_____

_____

_____

_____

_____

_____

_____

_____

_____

_____

Some **FADS**—
present and future

Today   **The 2000s**

_____   _____
_____   _____
_____   _____
_____   _____
_____   _____
_____   _____
_____   _____
_____   _____
_____   _____
_____   _____
_____   _____
_____   _____
_____   _____
_____   _____

SCHOOL IN THE NEXT MILLENNIUM

One thing is certain: In the next millennium, there will still be school. The school, however, will probably be a lot different from the school you go to now. You might even "go" to school without leaving home.

You've probably already guessed why experts think schools will change—computers. Maybe you don't have any of these machines in your school, or maybe you have a few in each classroom or a computer lab or library—some schools already have lots of computers. But in the future, computers in schools will probably be as common as chalkboards are today.

Imagine what a typical day in the school of the future might be like:

You carry your laptop computer to school with you. It can connect to the computer network at school, and it is programmed to recognize your face and your voice. Of course, it also has a keyboard.

The computer keeps a file of all your work. The teacher still talks to the class but also communicates with each student via computer. When students have questions about the lesson, they can enter them in the computer. Then the teacher will reply by sending individual answers to each student's laptop. This system makes it easier for everyone to work at his or her own pace. You can even quiz yourself and get help when you need it, because the computer tells you right away whether your answer is correct or not.

You can ask the computer—maybe even by voice—about a subject, such as the invention of the automobile. The computer knows which books, if any, you have already read on the topic. It can also coordinate what you are learning in school with your particular interests. For example, if you like classic cars or racing cars, the computer will display information about them. It might describe the first car radio and even play the first song ever played on a car radio.

In the school library, you can research a report using CD-ROMs or the Internet. You can put together a project that's almost like your own movie, with computer graphics and music—even a famous author's voice downloaded from the Internet.

You and your friends can use your computers to check out what's for lunch in the school cafeteria. If you need permission to go on a field trip, your parents can e-mail their consent right to the school.

By the way, instead of passing notes, you can send e-mail to your friends. But the teacher can monitor this through the computer network, so watch out! The teacher can use e-mail to send notes and your report card directly to your parents. Good luck!

Even though it is likely that kids will actually "go" to school in the next millennium, there might be times when they will just "tune in" to lessons at home. A student will probably talk to the teacher and other students through the school's computer network. Kids might even talk to teachers and students at other schools over the Internet. And maybe, just maybe, students will be able to talk to a teacher who is on another planet.

Of course, the computer won't replace other types of learning. Just the way seeing a delicious-looking pizza on a computer screen isn't like eating the pizza, seeing a science experiment on the computer or watching a video of how a papier-mâché mask is made won't take the place of actually doing the projects.

Here's an interesting idea. What if people didn't even have to use a computer to learn lessons? What if there was a way to plug information into our brains, the way we load a CD-ROM into a computer? Take some time to list your thoughts about this idea and other possibilities for school in the next millennium on page 18.

My thoughts about SCHOOL
in the next millennium:

_____

_____

_____

_____

_____

_____

_____

_____

_____

_____

_____

_____

_____

_____

_____

_____

YOU NAME IT

What's so special about names? Way back in the sixteenth century the famous playwright William Shakespeare answered this question in his play *Romeo and Juliet*:

> What's in a name? that which we call a rose
> By any other name would smell as sweet.

Do you agree with him? Would a rose be as appealing if it were called a barf bag?

Anyway, it seems that names can be important. Your name becomes part of who you are, doesn't it? Have you ever met someone who "looks like a 'Kathy'" or "looks like a 'Jason'"?

Do you like your own name? What about your best friend's name? Do you have a favorite name? Did you ever want to change yours?

If you've ever thought about changing your name, maybe a look at the following names that were given to real people will make you think again.

CORA APPLE	IMA HOGG
MAY B. DUNN	IONA OUTHOUSE
VIRGINIA HAM	TINEY BUGG

Lots of names have been around for centuries and have special meanings. Modern names also have special significance. Here are a few names and their meanings:

＊**DIANA**: In ancient Rome, the goddess of the
       moon was named Diana.
＊**LEO**: In Latin, "leo" means "lion."
＊**AISHA**: An African name that means "life."
＊**BEAU**: In French, "beau" means "handsome."
＊**SARAH**: A Hebrew name that means "princess."
＊**ANDREW**: A Greek name that means "manly."
＊**BRIAN**: A Celtic name that means "strong."

Before we start imagining what names will be popular in the next millennium, let's consider some names that aren't used much anymore and some that are currently popular.

We can begin with the names of some past presidents: for example, George Washington, John Adams, Thomas Jefferson, and James Buchanan. The names George, John, Thomas, and James are still quite popular. But what about Millard Fillmore, Ulysses S. Grant, Rutherford B. Hayes, and Woodrow Wilson? Have you met many people named Millard, Ulysses, Rutherford, or Woodrow lately? Probably not.

It's a fact that names go in and out of style. For instance, Mary was probably the most popular girl's name for the first fifty years of the twentieth century, but by 1975 it had dropped way down on the popularity scale. At that time, names like Michelle, Heather, Rebecca, Jennifer, Amy, and Melissa became popular.

While lots of girls were named Agnes back in 1875, not many are today.

What about boys' names? John has remained popular throughout this century, but in the past twenty-five years Jason, Matthew, Michael, Christopher, and Brian have become increasingly popular.

People choose names from all sorts of places. Sometimes they use the name of a family member or a friend. Names also come from popular songs and movies. The name Anastasia, for example, became a lot more popular after the movie of that name came out.

In the United States we have lots of interesting names from a variety of countries and cultures. It's not unusual to find Jessica, Juan, Keesha, Hai Jun, and Mikhail in the same classroom—although each of these names originated in a different country. In the near future, this variety is sure to increase. But in the United States right now, that is, the late 1990s, the ten most popular girls' and boys' names are as follows:

GIRLS	BOYS
Brittany	Michael
Ashley	Christopher
Jessica	Matthew
Amanda	Joshua
Sarah	Andrew
Megan	James
Kaitlin	John
Samantha	Nicholas
Stephanie	Justin
Katherine	David

Now let's think about the names people may have after the year 2000. What will the names of the creatures we may meet on other planets be like?

Just for fun, we can look at some of the names used in science fiction. Remember *Star Trek?* Well, there was a human character named Captain Kirk, but the aliens were called Dar, Korrod, and Sybok. People of the Klingon race had different kinds of names from those of the Vulcans, who were from another planet.

Remember some of the names from *Star Wars?* Chewbacca and Obi-Wan Kenobi? How about the robots, R2-D2 and C-3PO? And do you remember Gartogg, Jabba the Hutt, and Nien Nunb?

You might meet all kinds of people—and creatures—in the twenty-first century. Think about what names might be popular—for humans *and* aliens. List them on the following page. Then make a list of your current favorite names.

NAMES I think will
be popular in the 21st century—and beyond

_____   _____

_____   _____

_____   _____

_____   _____

_____   _____

_____   _____

_____   _____

My favorite names

_____   _____

_____   _____

_____   _____

_____   _____

_____   _____

_____   _____

FOOD IN THE NEXT MILLENNIUM

How will food change as we jump into the first century of the next millennium? At the beginning of the twentieth century, we didn't have nearly as many choices about what to eat as we do now. There weren't even any supermarkets back then.

Crackers were not packaged in little boxes. They were bought from a big barrel at the local store. Sugar and flour were bought the same way. There was no such thing as frozen food. People didn't have cake mixes. They put together eggs, flour, baking powder, and other ingredients to make cakes from "scratch," and then they baked them in the oven.

Of course, you can still make a cake this way—but look at all the other choices you have! You can buy a mix, add eggs and oil, and bake the ingredients in the oven or the microwave. You can buy the cake frozen, defrost it, and eat it. Or you can buy it frozen and bake it in an oven or a microwave. You can even buy a pastry and pop it in the toaster.

What about other ways to prepare food? If you've ever gone camping, you know that you can bring little packets of freeze-dried food, add water, and enjoy a meal. (That's a little like the way astronauts prepare their food in space.) Instead of popping popcorn in a pan on the stove the way people used to make it, you can use a special popcorn popper. You can buy a bag of already-popped corn, ready to eat. Or you can buy popcorn that can be cooked in the microwave and make it almost instantly so it's hot and fresh at home.

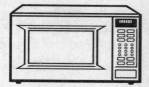

We now know more about other cultures than ever before, and we've become more interested in and accepting of the diverse cultures that are part of our country. Knowing how other people prepare food has given us many more choices about what to eat. Global communication networks send information instantly to all parts of the world, and air travel makes it possible for us to go anywhere in the world. It also means that food can be transported around the world quickly.

How have the developments of the twentieth century changed our eating habits? Now you can eat sushi, which has long been popular in Japan but was unavailable in the United States until only a few decades ago. You can also enjoy burritos and quesadillas, which are popular in Mexico, along with other foods from many different countries. Because of improved transportation, consumers in the United States can buy many more kinds of fresh fruits and vegetables all year round than ever before.

If you don't feel like cooking a meal, you can call a restaurant on the telephone and have food delivered. (Don't you love ordering pizza?) You can even look at a restaurant's menu on the Internet and place your order by e-mail. Or you can fax an order right to the restaurant.

Today, the food is delivered by a person in a car or truck. But maybe in the next millennium it will be delivered by a robot!

Now think about the *way* people eat. It often reflects the way they live and the kind of work they do. For example, when people had to do hard physical work on the farm, they got up early and prepared big meals that they ate by the time the sun came up. These meals might look like giant dinners to you—meat, pancakes, potatoes, pies, and cakes. You'd probably never dream of eating all that for breakfast—unless, of course, you lived on a farm. But there are not nearly as many people working on farms now as there used to be.

Because people today are busy doing a wide variety of things, many of us eat on the run. We eat lots of little snacks, and even when we eat a full meal, we don't spend much time preparing it. We look for ways to make food faster to prepare and faster to eat.

Let's see if our observations about eating habits can help predict what food will be like in the next millennium. What if you could fax an order to an instant pizza machine instead of a restaurant? You could order the pizza just the way you like it—thin or thick crust, extra cheese, any kind of topping—and send the order via fax or computer. A robot would deliver the hot, fresh pizza to your door. When you paid for the food, you wouldn't use cash. You'd use a computer—called a "pocket PC" or a "smart card"—that was programmed to keep track of what you spent.

Of course, fast food won't be all there is to eat in the 2000s, and people will have lots of other food-related problems to solve. Currently, we are becoming more health-conscious, and this trend is likely to continue. We're concerned about how the environment affects the food we eat. We don't want food that has been sprayed with harmful chemicals or grown in soil that is contaminated with poisons.

If we eat meat, we want to know that the animals were treated well and not fed harmful chemicals that will be passed on to us. And what exactly did they eat? Was it grass or grains grown pesticide-free? Was the water they drank free of chemicals? Not long ago it would have been difficult for consumers to get this kind of information. Now, thanks to computers, we can log on to the Internet and have most of our questions answered in a short time. So much information is available on the Internet, soon you'll be able to find out almost anything you want to know about companies that prepare the food.

What if you don't want to buy food from a company that also produces cigarettes or makes pesticides? What if you don't want to buy from a company that isn't responsible about recycling or waste disposal? What if you prefer not to support a company that contributes to research that hurts animals? It's very possible that you'll be able to find these things out via your computer in the near future.

Because there will be so many choices and so

much information available, every company that makes food will want to do its best to give customers what they want. You'll be able to share your opinion about which food products are good or bad by posting the information on computer bulletin boards.

You can already use the Internet to find out about the fat, calories, and other contents of most foods, but maybe in the future you'll be able to find out where the food you want was grown, how it was shipped to the store, and how long it has been sitting on the shelf—all before you even walk into the store.

As for your health, perhaps a computer in your home could tell you each day exactly what your body needs. Maybe the computer would detect that you're coming down with a cold and give you advice about taking extra vitamins. Or it could tell your mom or dad that they'd better cut down on fat. Then it could determine the nutritional value of everything you ate during the day. It could tell you if you'd gotten everything you needed that day for your body to stay healthy.

Suppose you're having a test at school and are under more stress than usual. Your computer might tell you what you should eat. You might even be able to get food made specifically for your body's needs—after all, your body's needs are different from those of a baby's body. Your older or younger brothers and sisters, your parents, and your grandparents all need different nutrients than you do.

Some experts who try to predict the future think that we'll be able to control all of the conditions under which our food is grown. In that case we would be sure the food was free from chemicals and had the most vitamins. What if you could instantly test a hamburger to make sure it's safe to eat before you consume it?

Maybe in the future we will make food from some other substance. Think of fatless fat—olestra. Would you want to eat completely artificial food? What about food that includes medicine? Candy that prevents headaches? Pizza that prevents tooth decay? Hamburgers that are meatless but taste like meat and prevent sore throats?

Maybe in the near future smart business people will open fast-food chains offering menus that meet your changing nutritional demands: for example, sandwiches made of free-range chicken and tofu-based recipes. But remember, because there will be more and more choices, the food will have to taste good, too.

What about food from other planets? And what about growing *our* food on other planets? Would you like to try to eat what aliens eat? Try planning the menu for a party in the next millennium by answering the questions on the following page.

PARTY MENU—
21ST CENTURY

You give a party sometime in the next millennium and invite not only Earthlings, but also aliens and robots. What will you serve? How will it be prepared? How will you shop for it?

_____

_____

_____

_____

_____

_____

_____

_____

_____

_____

_____

_____

_____

_____

SOLVING & PREVENTING CRIME IN THE NEXT MILLENNIUM

Of course our society is interested in solving crimes. Ideally, however, in the next millennium we'll shift the emphasis to preventing crime.

Many people think the attitudes that encourage crime will change for the better. Already there is a trend toward people caring more about each other, talking about prejudice, and trying to eliminate it. Many of us are looking for ways to solve problems without violence. You'll be part of building a future where crime might even be rare.

For now, let's look at some state-of-the-art crime-solving methods that are used today. You probably know all about fingerprints. No two people's prints are exactly alike, and for years law enforcement officers have been able to identify criminals by using fingerprints. But did you know about DNA fingerprinting—also called genetic fingerprinting?

We can think of DNA as the map, or blueprint, of heredity. Every baby inherits about half of its DNA from its mother, and about half from its father.

DNA appears in the nucleus, or center, of every cell in our bodies except red blood cells. That's because red blood cells don't have a nucleus. Most of the cells with nuclei contain twenty-three pairs of chromosomes. These chromosomes are bundles of DNA and contain our genes. Genes carry coded messages that determine whether you are short or tall, whether you have blue eyes or brown. They also determine the details that make you unique from every other human being alive.

All human beings have many traits in common: We all have muscles, brains, bones, a heart, and other shared characteristics. So, large strands of DNA are the same in all of us. But there is also some DNA that makes each one of us unique right down to our molecules.

What does DNA have to do with solving crimes? Well, DNA is found in some components of our blood. Chemicals can be used to separate the DNA from other substances, such as red blood cells, which don't contain DNA. Then the sample is analyzed to get a DNA print, which looks a little like a card with holes punched in it.

The DNA print made from blood samples, or from hair and skin cells taken from a crime scene, can be compared with the same kinds of samples taken from a crime suspect. If the two prints match, it's very strong evidence that the suspected criminal is guilty. If the two DNA prints don't match, then the DNA test can support a suspect's claim of innocence.

Use of DNA prints as legal evidence is still fairly new. Many law enforcement officials are wary of its accuracy, but others think the technology will be perfected.

Some people think that taking DNA prints of all babies shortly after birth would make it easier to find missing children. Information about every person could eventually be stored in computer files and made available to law enforcement officials all over the world.

Other experts think that taking DNA prints of each person is a bad idea. They think it is a mistake to keep a file of information about private citizens because this could lead to a violation of our right to privacy.

Here are some other crime-solving techniques:

*EXAMINING A HUMAN SKELETON—A person's skeleton can reveal important information about him or her. For example, the sex and approximate age of the person, and the cause of death. This information can lead to clues about the person's friends and enemies.

*BALLISTICS—The word means "the study of the flight of objects through space." When crime solvers use the term, they are referring to the investigation of bullets shot from guns used to commit crimes. When a bullet travels down the barrel of a gun, scratches are made on it. The scratches on the bullets shot from each gun are different. By studying bullets found at a crime scene, police can gather valuable clues about the weapon and from that, perhaps, who committed the crime.

✳FORENSIC ENTOMOLOGY—We now have lots of chemical methods to test if there is poison in a body. But there's another kind of testing that makes it possible for bugs to help us solve crimes. It's called the science of forensic entomology, and it's only a few decades old. This science makes use of the fact that bugs follow a strict timetable and tend to stay near their homes. If a city-dwelling bug is found on a body in the country, police may have good reason to suspect that the body has been moved. Bugs may not go near a body if the weather is too hot or too cold, so analyzing the bugs on a body can help determine the time of death.

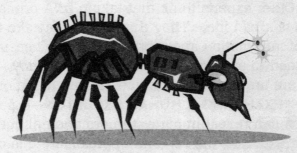

Aren't you surprised at all the crime-solving techniques we already have? Think about lie detector tests and checking telephone records to tell who called whom and when. Some people even think we can tell if someone is lying by watching the way he or she moves his or her eyes.

What's next? Robots are already being used as night watchmen and to help build cars—and even to explore other planets. A government agency is experimenting with small robots called RAPTORs that have the brains of desktop computers plus sensors that can be used to guard property. A group of small RAPTORs can be used to protect an area: One senses the motion of an intruder; another uses heat sensors to detect body warmth and send signals to still another robot that has a camera to transmit videotaped pictures back to headquarters. The technology to do this already exists.

We all know about home alarm systems and car alarms. Some cars even tell a thief to back off. Some store alarms send signals to services that contact the police and call the owner at home. What about a house that not only has an alarm, but also is equipped with an audio system that warns burglars to get away?

Movies—such as *Mission: Impossible*—can give us a glimpse into a possible future. In this action thriller, an organization tries to prevent break-ins by identifying employees by fingerprints, by voice prints, by eye scanning, and by heat sensors that reveal if more than one body is in a room. Wow!

In another thriller, *The Net,* a criminal breaks into private computer files and is able to make it look as if an innocent person has a criminal record. Because this information is sent to nationwide computer files, the innocent person's life is nearly destroyed.

Sadly, in the early years of the next millennium there will probably be more computer-related crimes. Computers are wonderful inventions, but they also have a down side. Criminals can break into computer systems and retrieve private information about people, such as their credit card numbers, telephone numbers, addresses, and medical records. Why is that so terrible? Well, for one thing, you should be able to decide who knows this personal information. Nobody should be allowed to find it out without your permission.

Another reason computer-related crimes are bad is because of something called *identity theft*. It's basically what happened in *The Net*. Somebody who gets your social security number, your credit card numbers, your bank card number, or your computer password can pretend to be you. The imposter can buy things in your name, and you'll have to pay for them—unless you can prove it wasn't really you who bought them. Identity theft has already happened to some people.

Let's hope that we will all work together to minimize crime in the next millennium and to make the world a safer place.

THERE WILL BE
MORE CRIME (OR LESS CRIME)
IN THE NEXT MILLENNIUM.
Choose one and explain your choice below.

_____

_____

_____

_____

_____

Possible
CRIME-SOLVING
TECHNIQUES
in the 21st century

_____

_____

_____

_____

_____

_____

THE HOME OF THE FUTURE

What will the home of the future be like? We can guess, but we can't know for sure. Let's look back at the 1950s and see what the people of that time thought homes would be like in the year 2000.

A magazine called *Popular Mechanics* featured an article about a make-believe community of the future called Tottenville. Life in Tottenville was supposed to imitate what life would be like in the next millennium.

Tottenville's airport was in the center of town. (Doesn't that seem kind of noisy to you?) There were plenty of parks and wide-open spaces, and you were considered a criminal if you polluted the air.

Although people were serious about preventing pollution in Tottenville, they weren't concerned about recycling or saving things. For example, there were no dishwashers in Tottenville, because dirty dishes were just thrown away!

Housecleaning in Tottenville sounds like an adventure. All you had to do was hose down the inside of the house. You didn't need to worry about ruining the furniture or the rugs because everything was waterproof.

When you finished cleaning the house, you turned off the hose and all the water ran down a drain. Then you dried everything off with a blast of hot air.

Preparing meals in Tottenville sounds like even more fun than housecleaning. The average meal was prepared in seventy-five seconds. Today we can't even manage that kind of speed with microwave cooking.

The inventors of Tottenville weren't all wrong about the future. They predicted that people would conduct business over television screens. They didn't call it telecommuting and didn't know about the Internet, but it seems like they were on the right track.

Why don't we try to predict the home of the future from our perspective today? We can get an idea of what life may be like in the new millennium by looking at the home of Bill Gates, who created the Microsoft Corporation. There's a lot of computer power in Mr. Gates's house, but you don't see these computers—you just experience what they can do for you.

When you go into Bill Gates's house, you can wear a special identification tag. A tiny computer inside the tag communicates with the computer network that controls the house. You can program your ID tag with all kinds of information, such as your favorite kinds of art and music, or the temperature you find the most comfortable. Then, as you walk through the house, you'll hear your favorite music and see your favorite kinds of art displayed on big video screens. You might want to see Leonardo Da Vinci's Mona Lisa, or modern art or photographs.

The cool thing about the house is that while you

are enjoying your favorite art and music, people in other rooms can watch and listen to *their* favorites.

Here's another amazing thing about Bill Gates's house. If you get a telephone call, the phone will ring only in the room where *you* are!

There's more: As you walk through the house, the lights automatically turn on when you enter a room and turn themselves off when you leave. That's if you need lights—the house knows that, too. It's a really "smart" house. When nobody is there or people are sleeping, the temperature decreases to save energy. For people who want to turn everything on and off themselves, there are switches that can override the computer.

Of course, you and your friends don't live in houses like this now. But since the technology already exists, it's possible that you may live in something similar in the next millennium. For example, television will be different. Already, you can choose from more channels, either on cable or via satellite, but television in the future will be interactive. That means, for example, you can watch a program when it suits you—without recording it—instead of just when it is being broadcast. Won't that be great?

Let's think about what your home of the future might be like. What kinds of electronic equipment will you use? What will your house look like? Will the rooms be heated by solar power? Take a few minutes to write down your thoughts.

My HOME in the 21st century

_____

_____

_____

_____

_____

_____

_____

_____

_____

_____

_____

_____

_____

_____

_____

_____

_____

SHOPPING IN THE NEXT MILLENNIUM

As you can probably imagine, shopping in the twenty-first century will be a lot different from the way we buy things today. Shopping is already changing rapidly, and the driving force behind these changes is—you guessed it—the computer. In the new millennium you'll probably get most things by ordering them from home through your computer. This is already happening thanks to the World Wide Web and the Internet. Many stores already have on-line shopping, and as we begin the new millennium the Internet will be crowded with more buying opportunities. As a result of this increased competition, people who make products will have to attract customers by offering the most appealing items at the best prices, because there will be so many choices.

Virtual reality is another idea that could dramatically change the future of shopping. You've probably played some sort of virtual-reality game, where you put on gloves and goggles and are projected into another world through computer imaging. This technology will become more and more sophisticated in the next millennium.

Imagine a virtual-reality computer screen that shows three-dimensional lifelike images. You can project an image of yourself onto the screen and "try on" clothes. You even change the design of the garment to better suit your body type and your tastes. For example, you might like this or that shirt without pockets, or with shorter or longer sleeves, add embroidery, and so on. The finished clothing is delivered to your home a few  weeks later—maybe in a truck driven by a robot. You could even use virtual reality to "walk around" a car to examine it before you test-drive it.

Let's consider the future of shopping malls. You know how much fun it is to hang out at the mall with your friends, but the malls of the future might be quite different. Why? Because more babies were born in the United States during the "baby boom"—roughly from 1946 to 1964—than at any other time. This means that it won't be long before there are more older people than younger people in the country. Maybe shopping malls will be geared for the older crowd, with more gyms and relaxation spas and fewer music stores and trendy clothing boutiques.

Another possibility is that stores and shopping malls will be more exciting than ever for all age groups. In order to get people to give up the convenience of ordering food and other products from home, many stores will have to woo customers to the mall by offering something special. Going to the mall may one day be a total entertainment experience, like going to a concert or visiting Disney World.

Customers will be encouraged to give their opinions to the store owners and to other customers. This will also motivate merchants to offer the best products at the best prices, so you may spend less on food, clothing, and other goods. Not a bad idea!

CENTURY SHOPPING MALL

Write about the ideal shopping mall of the future. Will robots guide you around? Will areas of the mall have different themes—a jungle safari or a street in Paris? Will you zoom through the stores on vehicles that fly?

_____

_____

_____

_____

_____

_____

_____

_____

_____

_____

_____

_____

TRAVEL IN THE TWENTY-FIRST CENTURY

The idea of civilians as well as astronauts traveling to other planets is exciting, but how well are we doing with travel right here on our own planet? People have finally realized that not only is burning certain kinds of fuel unhealthy for their bodies but it is also destroying Earth's atmosphere and polluting the water. It's likely that, in the future, corporations and individuals will be required to use only environmentally safe fuel—or maybe no fuel at all. Perhaps people will be driving electric cars, air-powered cars, or cars that use some other kind of power. You might even help develop this new energy source.

What if we discovered a substitute for cars? Just for a moment, let your imagination run wild. Maybe you can strap a power pack on your back that will enable you to zoom through the air. Maybe you can be instantly transported from place to place through some sort of invention not yet created.

Now let's go on to space travel! In 1969, humans finally landed on the moon. The *Apollo 11* spacecraft mission was launched on July 16, and it landed on the moon on July 20.

Lieutenant Neil A. Armstrong descended to the surface of the moon and said the historic words: "That's one small step for a man, one giant leap for mankind." It certainly was, considering that at the beginning of the twentieth century people were still traveling by horse and buggy, bicycles, and railway. Then came motor cars. In 1903, the Wright brothers launched the first gasoline-powered airplane, the *Flyer,* at Kitty Hawk, North Carolina. Most people thought air travel would never work.

Where will we go in the next millennium? We've learned a lot about our solar system, which is made up of the sun, nine planets (including Earth), their satellites, and asteroids, comets, dust, and gas. Whew!

Our galaxy is called the Milky Way. The sun and its planets are only part of this galaxy. It also includes all the stars you can see without a telescope. Beyond the Milky Way, there are thousands of other galaxies in the universe.

As we approach the twenty-first century, the progress we've made in space travel is impressive. Spacecraft have landed on the moon, Mars, and Venus. They have flown near Mercury, Jupiter, Saturn, Uranus, and Neptune. Satellites have been launched into space to study what's out there and to send information back to Earth.

If we continue this rate of progress, it's possible that you could travel to another planet in our solar system during your lifetime. Where do you think you might like to go?

Before you answer, let's consider what it's like at some other places in our solar system. The sun is a star, a big, shining concentration of gas. Since it's really hot and doesn't have a surface, landing on it would be impossible.

Mercury, Mars, and Venus are made up mostly of rock and iron. Maybe you'd like to explore one of those. The outer planets—Jupiter, Saturn, Uranus, and Neptune—are mostly hydrogen, helium, and ice. The farthest known planet in our solar system, Pluto, is the coldest one of all.

Our galaxy is huge, but we know that there are other galaxies in outer space too. Scientists use satellites with high-powered telescopes to locate planets light-years away from Earth. Perhaps they will discover intelligent life on one of these planets in the new millennium—and maybe aliens aren't quite as different from humans as we think!

MY BEST
(ALIEN) FRIEND

Suppose you have a best friend who just happens to be an alien. What does your friend look like? How did you meet, and how do you communicate? What is your friend's name? Does this alien have any special abilities, such as flying, mind reading, or seeing through walls?

_____

_____

_____

_____

_____

_____

_____

_____

_____

_____

_____

_____

MY ALIEN PET

Suppose you traveled to another planet, and an alien gave you a pet that you brought back to Earth. You are the only Earthling who can see the pet. Describe this creature. What problems might you encounter having an invisible pet?

_____

_____

_____

_____

_____

_____

_____

_____

_____

_____

_____

_____

_____

_____

MEDICAL BREAKTHROUGHS

In "Food in the Next Millennium," we imagined how a "smart" house might monitor your health and give you advice about vitamins and nutritional food. It's also possible that you will wear a tiny computer that contains your complete medical records, which doctors could instantly access in an emergency.

Not all the expectations for medicine in the millennium are computer-related. One area that's being seriously studied is the link between mind and body—that is, how your mood affects whether or not you get sick. Medical research has already established links between feeling sad and depressed and having higher rates of heart attacks. It has also established a link between feeling optimistic—hopeful—and surviving some types of surgery. It seems that happy people with strong connections to their family and communities tend to be in better health than those who are socially isolated. In the next millennium medical researchers may find out exactly how a person's emotional state and physical well-being are tied together.

Another exciting area of medical research is (back to computers again!) the merging of humans and machines—cybernetics. Doctors at the Harvard Medical

School are already putting a team together to build a bionic eye. The group expects that within five years it will conduct studies of computer chips implanted into human eyes. If the implants are successful, there may be a way to restore vision to the blind in the twenty-first century.

This opens up even more exciting possibilities. An artificial eye with superhuman capabilities, such as telescopic and microscopic vision, could be available during your lifetime. A cybernetic eye might be more powerful than the strongest human eye.

In the world beyond 2020, we may be able to connect artificial arms, legs, and eyes directly to the human nervous system. This would be a great help to people who have disabilities. Scientists say that it's still pretty much impossible to think of an entirely cybernetic human being anytime soon—but perhaps someday it will happen.

Another exciting medical possibility is the elimination of diseases at the genetic level. If we can find out what makes inherited diseases happen, we might be able to correct the conditions that cause the diseases before they can do any damage.

There's more. An amazing breakthrough was made near the end of the twentieth century, one that may change medical science in the future. A sheep named Dolly was cloned in Scotland in February 1997. What is cloning?

In "Solving & Preventing Crime in the Next Millennium" we talked about DNA and noted that no two people have the same DNA. But Dolly the sheep has the same DNA as another sheep, thanks to cloning. That means she is an exact duplicate, right down to her molecules. In August  1997 it was announced that a calf named Gene had been cloned. And in July 1998 a team of scientists used a new technique to clone more than 50 identical mice.

What does cloning mean for the future of medicine? Nobody is exactly sure. It's unlikely that a human being will ever be cloned. But through cloning experiments with animals scientists may one day discover a disease-preventing gene in DNA. If that happens, perhaps the gene can be cloned and given to sick people to make them well. And there may come a day when, thanks to cloning, scientists will be able to wipe out some of the most deadly diseases we know.

Take a few minutes and think about what you would like to accomplish if you became a doctor in the next millennium. Would you work on ridding the world of cancer and AIDS? Would you work on bionics?

What would I do as a DOCTOR
in the 21st century?

_____
_____
_____
_____
_____
_____
_____
_____
_____
_____
_____
_____
_____
_____
_____
_____
_____
_____
_____
_____
_____
_____

GLOOM AND DOOM

When the twentieth century dawned, people thought the future would be very bright. They were sure that life would keep getting better and better right through the year 2000.

By the middle of the twentieth century, however, attitudes had changed. Some people thought prosperity would continue, but others weren't so sure.

One major development that scared people was the creation of weapons of mass destruction. The atomic bomb was built in 1945. When it was dropped on Hiroshima, Japan, during World War II that same year, it completely destroyed the city.

In 1952 an even more powerful bomb was made: the hydrogen bomb. One hydrogen bomb was several times more destructive than an atomic bomb. In schools there were drills to practice what to do if a bomb exploded. About once a month children got under their desks and covered their heads in mock preparation for an air raid.

Another concern of people at the middle of the century was the expectation that by the year 2000 there would not be enough food for everyone on Earth. Production of food was not expected to keep up with the population explosion. Many people thought the solution to this problem would be to make food from other materials, such as wood pulp. They also thought it would be possible to recycle paper napkins and underwear into candy. Yuck!

There have been gloom-and-doom prophecies for centuries. Way back in the first half of the sixteenth century, a very famous prophet named Nostradamus had some ideas about the year 2000. He predicted that the end of the twentieth century would be rather grim, but that humankind would redeem itself in the next millennium and we could look forward to better times.

Nostradamus is famous because it seems that many things he said would happen did. He wasn't always right, but some of his predictions were surprisingly on target. For example, some people say he foretold the outbreak of World War II. Others believe he predicted the Great Fire of London in 1666 and the year of Queen Elizabeth I's death (1603). Apparently he even foretold the date of his own death!

The problem with trying to interpret Nostradamus's predictions is that he wrote them in rhyming verses, and his language was often vague. As a result, there are many interpretations for each of his prophecies, so we can never be entirely sure if they are true or not.

Don't worry about what Nostradamus said. Instead, try to create the most exciting future that your generation can imagine. Blast off into the year 2000!

LOOKING BACK

Take a few minutes to jot down your favorite people and things on the following pages. Save this book and look at it in a few years to see what you wrote. Have your tastes changed much?

My favorite **MOVIES** in 1999:

_____

_____

_____

_____

_____

_____

My favorite
MUSIC GROUPS
in 1999:

_____

_____

_____

_____

_____

_____

_____

Some of my favorite
ACTIVITIES
in 1999:

_____

_____

_____

_____

_____

_____

My
BEST FRIENDS
in 1999:

_____

_____

_____

_____

_____

_____

_____

MY LIFE IN THE MILLENNIUM

 What do you think your life will be like in the twenty-first century? Answer these questions and then write down any other ideas you have.

What job will you have?_____

_____

Will everyone have an electric car? _____

_____

Will everyone have a cell phone?_____

_____

Will you ever take a vacation using virtual reality?

_____

_____

Will you be married?_____

_____

Will you have children? _____

_____

Will you be famous? _____

_____

Will you travel to another planet? _____

_____

Will you meet a space alien? _____

_____

What do you think your life will be like? _____

_____

_____

_____

_____

_____

_____

DECEMBER 31, 1999

Think of it. There won't be another New Year's Eve like this one for one thousand years. And you're right in the middle of it.

New Year's Eve is usually a good reason for a big party. This new year will be an excuse for a stupendous, mega-gigantic party all over the world. How do you think people will celebrate it? See if any of these ideas sounds like a great way to celebrate. Check the ones you like best.

_____ Travel to Europe on the Concorde with a group of your friends and have a huge party in a foreign country.

_____ Have a group of your friends over for a party and spend some of the time on the Internet, chatting with other kids from all over the world.

_____ Go to an observatory, have a party there, and look up at the stars.

_____ Fly to Egypt and begin the new year at the pyramids of Giza.

_____ Ring in the new millennium at the huge Millennium Dome on the Prime Meridian in Greenwich, England.

_____ Turn on the television and watch the new millennium begin on each continent.

_____ Head to Times Square in New York City and watch with millions of other people as the Millennium Ball drops.

_____ Make a time capsule containing special mementos of who you are right now. When the clock strikes midnight, seal the capsule and put it away for five or ten years. When you open it, the world—and you—will have changed.

Write down a few of your own ideas for celebrating the new millennium:

_____

_____

_____

_____

_____

NEW YEAR'S RESOLUTIONS SCORECARD

On January 1, 2000, write down your resolutions for the first year of the new millennium. In December 2000, look back and find out how many resolutions you kept.

January 2000 Resolutions	Was this resolution kept?
_____	_____
_____	_____
_____	_____
_____	_____
_____	_____
_____	_____
_____	_____
_____	_____
_____	_____